ISLAND
ALPHABET

An ABC of Maine Islands

*Written and Illustrated
by Kelly Paul Briggs*

Down East Books
Camden, Maine

Copyright © 1995 by Kelly Paul Briggs
ISBN 0-89272-369-6
Text and jacket design by Eugenie Seidenberg Delaney
Color separations by High Resolution, Inc., Camden, Me.
Printed and bound at Everbest Printing, Hong Kong, through
Four Colour Imports, Louisville, Ky.

1 3 5 4 2

Down East Books / Camden, Maine

For Don, with love.

Within this little book of Maine
are many islands, wild and tame.
So, come with me and take a peek—
I'm sure you'll find each one unique!

A is for ALLEN,
a cross it does bear,
to mark the first Anglican
service held there.

Captain George Weymouth anchored his ship *Archangel* at Allen
Island, offshore from the mouth of the St. George River, in May
1605. He and his crew held a Whitsunday church service there, the
first Anglican service in New England. A stone cross on the island still
marks the event.

B is for BRIMSTONE,
whose shiny black stones
are covered in snow
when the winter wind moans.

Perhaps best known for the beautiful black stones on their shores, Brimstone and Little Brimstone Islands are owned by The Nature Conservancy. Leach's storm petrels, rare nocturnal sea birds that come ashore only to breed, nest there all summer.

C — COMPASS Island
was known once before
as Turnip because these
were washed up on shore.

Legend has it that a schooner named *Jackie* was shipwrecked off
Pulpit Rock many years ago, and spilled its cargo of turnips on this
island, which then became known as Turnip Island. Later, the name
was changed to Compass, probably marking the island's navigational
usefulness.

D for DEER ISLE,
where the fishing boats roam
from Stonington Harbor,
the port they call home.

Fishing has always been important on Deer Isle, but granite was
also quarried here in the nineteenth century. Some of the stone for the
George Washington Bridge, Rockefeller Center, the Smithsonian
Institution, and the John F. Kennedy Memorial came from Deer Isle.

E — ENSIGN Island,
still wild in its ways,
was too small for farming
in earlier days.

Ensign and Little Ensign Islands are too small to support
habitation, so they were never settled. Early this century, they were
owned by artist Charles Dana Gibson, who built his summer home on
neighboring Seven Hundred Acre Island. His wife, Irene Langhorne,
was the "Gibson girl" model.

F is for FISHERMAN.
On it does stand
a cottage where birds
are now welcome to land.

The fishermen who used to camp on Fisherman Island tried to
destroy the nests of sea birds because they thought the birds ate too
many fish. Later, the State of Maine purchased the island, and now
protects it for nesting eider ducks, cormorants, gulls, and guillemots.

G is for GRAFFAM,
beside it is Bar.
It's close to the mainland—
the sail is not far.

Graffam Island was purchased in 1857 for its granite, but the
owner died before any quarries were developed. At low tide, a sand
spit connects Graffam Island to nearby Bar Island, where beach-
combers look for sand dollars and other treasures. Though it is close
to the mainland, Graffam has never had year-round residents.

H is for HURRICANE.
Granite was found
and mined on this island
before Outward Bound.

The Hurricane Island quarries were worked for about forty years, and the granite helped build the St. Louis Post Office, the Boston Art Museum, the Metropolitan Museum of Art, and the Treasury Building in Washington, D.C. Since 1964, the island has been leased to the Outward Bound School.

I, for ISLESBORO,
where land was once sought
by summer folks coming
on steamer and yacht.

In the late 1800s, summer "rusticators" began buying Islesboro
farms and turning them into grand summer estates. Many island
residents then stopped fishing and farming and instead worked as
builders, boat captains, and caretakers for the summer people.

J is for JOB, which was
once known as Long.
For decades, its island
traditions stayed strong.

(Job is pronounced with a long O.) While nearby Islesboro and
Seven Hundred Acre Island became colonies for summer visitors, the
people on Job Island carried on in a more traditional way. Clamming,
lobstering, and sheep farming remained strong family businesses there
up until the middle of this century.

K is for KIMBALL,
where Seaside Farm Inn,
housed summer guests
'til the year 1910.

In the 1880s, when Isle au Haut was experiencing a tourist
boom, Benjamin Smith followed the trend by remodeling his farm
and advertising for guests. His inn was called Seaside Farm and was
the longest-running summer inn of the area. It closed in 1910.

L is for LIME,
with its bold rugged coast,
its long, varied past,
and its lime kilns to boast.

In the late 1770s, Lime Island's kilns sent lime down the bay to
Castine, and other towns, where it was used to make fertilizer, plaster,
mortar for laying brick, and whitewash. Later, the lime business
declined, the kilns were abandoned, and the island returned to its
natural state.

M — MOUNT DESERT,
with Mount Cadillac's view,
and sheer cliffs, and beaches,
and woods to walk through.

(There are two ways to pronounce the name. For this rhyme, say "Mount *Dessert*.") More than a hundred years ago Mount Desert Island became a popular summer resort. Land bought and donated to the government by wealthy summer residents was the beginning of today's Acadia National Park.

N, for NORTH HAVEN,
an island retreat
with snug coves and harbors
where boaters can meet.

North Haven's summer community, one of the first in America,
was founded by a Boston yachtsman who saw that the sheltered waters
around the island were ideal for racing small boats. The Fox Island
Thorofare, the beautiful stretch of water between North Haven and
Vinalhaven Islands, is one of Maine's favorite cruising grounds.

O is for OTTER,
an island whose name
comes from this mammal
and its playful game.

Otter Island sits a few miles from Allen Island, in Muscongus Bay.
Schooners sometimes anchored for the night in a secluded cove on the
southwest side. In recent years, river otters have been spotted here, and
no doubt the island took its name from earlier such inhabitants.

P is for PLEASANT.
A small cobble beach
shapes cozy Home Harbor—
quite easy to reach.

Like its neighbors, Hewitt and Graffam, Pleasant Island has been the summer home of lobstermen and their families since early this century. Today, only a couple of families spend the summer here. Home Harbor is seldom used, and Cobble Beach is a nice place to row ashore.

Q is for QUARRIES.
In reading you'll find
no fewer than thirty-five
islands were mined.

At least 35 Maine islands were once mined for granite. The stone was used for paving, mooring blocks, curbstones, headstones, horse troughs, and pillars. Schooners transported the granite to distant cities to be used in projects such as Grant's Tomb, the Brooklyn Bridge, and the Statue of Liberty.

R is for RAM,
of the Islesboro group.
By these rocky isles
has sailed many a sloop.

There are several Ram islands along the Maine coast. One of
them is part of an island cluster called the Islesboro group. It lies near
the northern side of Islesboro, just beyond Flat and Seal Islands,
welcoming schooners and other boats as they pass up and down the bay.

S, for SEAL Island.
On this remote land,
burrows for puffins
have been dug by hand.

During World War II, Seal Island was used as a bombing range. A fire in 1978 burned over half the island, disrupting the island's nesting birds and exploding old bombshells left over from wartime. Since then, people from the National Audubon Society have dug nesting burrows for puffins so they will nest on Seal Island once again.

T is for TEEL,
where the Teel family tree
spanned five generations—
a long history.

King George II granted this island to Adam Teel, and it remained
in the Teel family for about 140 years. Henry Teel was the last to live
there. After Henry died, none of the younger family members wanted
to take over the island, so it was sold. Artist Andrew Wyeth once
painted Henry Teel looking out to sea from his kitchen window.

U — On UPPER GOOSE Island,
great blue herons nest.
Their rookery here
is the largest and best.

The Nature Conservancy owns Upper Goose, a 94-acre wooded
island on the western side of Middle Bay. The largest great blue heron
rookery in New England is established here. More than 250 nests have
been counted in the island's hemlock, beech, and yellow birch trees.

V—VINALHAVEN
holds legend and lore.
The *Royal Tar* burned one night
off its lee shore.

In October 1836, after touring New Brunswick, Canada, a circus embarked on the steamer *Royal Tar.* Strong winds and a fire on board sent 72 passengers, 20 crewmen, and camels, lions, circus horses, a leopard, a Bengal tiger, a gnu, and an elephant named "Mogul" into the water near the island of Vinalhaven.

W, for WARREN,
an island state park.
A great place to sail
should one choose to embark.

Warren Island, inhabited until the turn of the century, was later
acquired by the State of Maine. It is now a state park. Warren has a
beautiful cove for dropping anchor, a perfect place to row ashore, walk
the trails, toast marshmallows, and camp out under the stars.

X is for XMAS Cove,
miles from Port Clyde
on Monhegan Island—
a ferry boat's ride.

Christmas ("Xmas") Cove is on the southern end of Monhegan Island, about ten miles from the mainland. A mail boat makes daily runs from Port Clyde to this beautiful island, where cliffs tower 160 feet above the sea, the highest on America's east coast.

Y is for YORK Island,
near Isle au Haut.
Where now only sheep graze—
one hundred or so.

Patrick Conley bought York Island in 1847, and it remained in the
Conley family for a century. The family raised sheep, built homes, and
rented out cabins to fishermen. Summer visitors still come to York
Island, and sheep still live there. (Maine speakers use the English
pronunciation of *isle* for Isle au Haut.)

Z is for UNCLE ZEKE'S,
in Casco Bay.
It's too far to sail now—
let's call it a day!

Uncle Zeke's is a tiny island in the upper part of Harpswell Sound, north of Orrs Island. It has no trees, but sea birds nest in the bushes and grass there.

THANK YOU to Jo Ellen McAllister Stammen for her encouragement and artistic guidance from the very beginning of this project.

I'm grateful to Terry and Ned Gruener for their helpful critiques and unfailing support, to Frank Simon for taking me to the islands on a blustery November day, and to Judy Barstow for lending me photographs and books. Peter Stevick, at College of the Atlantic, and Brad Allan, of the Maine Department of Inland Fisheries & Wildlife, helped me with factual information. Thanks are also due to Jean Geiger, who let me sketch Uncle Zeke's Island from her back porch, and especially to my mother, librarian Diane Paul, who provided an enormous amount of reference material, from A to Z!